A VIEWERS GUIDE TO THE BOY AND THE HERON

A Comprehensive Guide to understanding Miyazaki's cinematic masterpiece.

Charles Kenny

A VIEWERS GUIDE TO

THE BOY AND THE HERON

Copyright © 2023 by Charles Kenny

All rights reserved. No part of this publication may be reproduced, distributed, or transmitted in any form or by any means, including photocopying, recording, or other electronic or mechanical methods, without the prior written permission of the publisher, except in the case of brief quotations embodied in critical reviews and certain other noncommercial uses permitted by copyright law.

DEDICATION

Dedicated to the visionary creator, Hayao Miyazaki, and the exceptional team behind *The Boy and The Heron*. His unparalleled storytelling and their collective artistry have given life to a cinematic masterpiece. He and his team's dedication to craft have woven a tale that transcends time, leaving an indelible mark on the world of animation.

TABLE OF CONTENT

Introduction

Chapter One
  The Context

Chapter Two
  Exploring the Plot

Chapter Three

Chapter Four
  Behind the Scenes

Chapter Five
  The Voice Cast

Chapter Six
  Themes and Motifs

Chapter Seven
  Music and Soundtrack

Chapter Eight
  Release and Reception

Chapter Nine

Impact on Pop Culture

Introduction

The Boy and the Heron movie, an animated masterpiece, is a captivating tale rooted in the life of a 12-year-old boy named Mahito Maki. At its core, the story revolves around Mahito's journey after a tragic incident that changes the course of his life forever: the loss of his mother. This poignant narrative not only explores Mahito's personal growth but also delves into broader themes, incorporating the rich storytelling style that has become synonymous with the works of renowned animator Hayao Miyazaki.

Mahito's story is one of resilience, courage, and self-discovery. In the face of adversity, he embarks on a transformative quest, navigating a world filled with both beauty and challenges. The film is a testament to the human spirit and the ability to find hope and meaning even in the darkest moments.

In this comprehensive guide, we'll unravel the layers of The Boy and the Heron, providing readers with a deeper understanding of the movie's origins, its narrative intricacies, and the creative genius behind it. We'll explore the historical context that inspired Miyazaki's storytelling, shedding light on the Pacific War's impact on Japan and how these real-world events shaped the fictional world of Mahito Maki.

As we journey through the plot, we'll analyze key moments and characters, unraveling the symbolism woven into the fabric of the story. Mahito Maki's path is not only a personal one but also a reflection of Miyazaki's own experiences, adding a layer of authenticity and depth to the narrative. The supporting cast, including the enigmatic Grey Heron and Mahito's companions like Natsuko and Shoichi, will be examined to uncover their roles in shaping the protagonist's destiny.

Behind the scenes, we'll explore Miyazaki's decision to come out of retirement for this particular project, providing insights into the creative process that brought The Boy and the Heron to life. From concept to completion, we'll delve into the challenges faced during production and how the team overcame them, giving readers a glimpse into the making of this cinematic gem.

The voice cast, both in the original Japanese version and the English adaptation, will be under the spotlight. We'll analyze the performances that breathe life into the characters and discuss how the choice of voice actors contributes to the overall viewing experience.

Themes and motifs play a crucial role in Miyazaki's films, and The Boy and the Heron is no exception. We'll explore the autobiographical elements in the movie, dissect the central theme of creating a world without conflict, and interpret the diverse layers of meaning woven into the narrative.

Music has always been a hallmark of Studio Ghibli films, and we'll dedicate a section to Joe Hisaishi's enchanting score and Kenshi Yonezu's evocative theme song, "Chikyūgi" (Spinning Globe). We'll discuss how the soundtrack enhances the emotional impact of the film, making it a memorable auditory experience.

Release and reception, impact on pop culture, and the movie's lasting legacy will also be explored. From box office performance to critical acclaim and fan reactions on social media, we'll paint a comprehensive picture of The Boy and the Heron's place in the world of cinema.

As we conclude, we'll recap key insights, celebrate the enduring impact of The Boy and the Heron, and encourage readers to delve deeper into the magic of Miyazaki's cinematic universe. This guide is a companion for both newcomers and ardent fans, inviting them to embark on a journey of understanding and appreciation for one of Studio Ghibli's most remarkable creations.

Chapter One
The Context

The Boy and the Heron is no exception, and its narrative is intricately connected to the post-World War II era in Japan. At the heart of the story lies the character of Mahito Maki, a 12-year-old boy whose life takes a drastic turn after the loss of his mother. Miyazaki, known for his ability to blend fantasy with reality, weaves a tale that reflects not only personal struggles but also the collective trauma of a nation recovering from the aftermath of war.

The Pacific War, which unfolded from 1941 to 1945, had a profound impact on Japan, both socially and culturally. The scars of conflict were still fresh, and the country was undergoing a period of reconstruction. Against this historical backdrop, Miyazaki introduces Mahito as a symbol of resilience, embodying the spirit of a nation determined to rebuild and find hope in the midst of adversity.

The choice of a heron as a central motif in the film is laden with symbolism. In Japanese culture, the heron is often associated with longevity, purity, and good fortune. However, it is also a creature that thrives in both water and air, symbolizing the dual nature of life—filled with both challenges and moments of soaring triumph. As Mahito navigates his own journey, the heron becomes a metaphor for the ebb and flow of life, resonating with audiences on a symbolic level that transcends cultural boundaries.

Miyazaki's decision to explore the impact of war on children is a poignant one. Mahito's coming-of-age story mirrors the collective experience of a generation that grew up against the backdrop of conflict. The film becomes a reflection on the resilience of youth, the power of imagination as a coping mechanism, and the importance of preserving innocence in the face of a changing world.

In this section, we will explore the historical events that influenced Miyazaki's storytelling, shedding light on the director's intention to create a narrative that goes beyond entertainment. By understanding the context of post-war Japan and the societal shifts that occurred during that period, viewers gain a deeper appreciation for the layers of meaning woven into The Boy and the Heron.

Additionally, we'll examine the cultural nuances embedded in the film. From traditional rituals to the representation of nature, every element is a deliberate choice that contributes to the overall atmosphere and thematic resonance. This exploration of context is an invitation to view The Boy and the Heron as more than just an animated feature; it is a cinematic reflection on the human condition, framed within the historical and cultural canvas of post-war Japan.

Chapter Two
Exploring the Plot

In the turbulent backdrop of 1943, amidst the chaos of the Pacific War, the tale of The Boy and the Heron unfolds, centering around 12-year-old Mahito Maki. The story kicks off with a heartbreaking event – the tragic death of Mahito's mother, Hisako, in a Tokyo hospital fire. A year later, Mahito's father, Shoichi, seeks solace in a new marriage with Hisako's younger sister, Natsuko. The family, including several aging maids, relocates to Natsuko's countryside estate, setting the stage for a narrative filled with grief, mystery, and magical realism.

Mahito, grappling with the loss of his mother, finds himself in an unfamiliar town. His struggles intensify as he contends with the persistent presence of a mysterious grey heron at the estate, a creature that becomes a symbol of both curiosity and torment. Meanwhile, his relationship with Natsuko, now carrying the weight of pregnancy, adds tension to the family dynamic.

The young protagonist's journey takes an unexpected turn when he discovers a sealed tower in the nearby woods. Drawn to the heron's elusive antics, Mahito fashions a bow and arrow from its feathers, setting the stage for a series of revelations that will shape his destiny.

As Mahito copes with the challenges of his new life, a pivotal moment occurs when, in a fit of despair, he purposefully injures himself. Recovering at the estate, he stumbles upon a novel titled How Do You Live?, bearing his mother's handwriting. This poignant discovery provides a connection to his mother and foreshadows the magical journey that lies ahead.

The plot thickens as Natsuko goes missing, prompting Mahito and one of the maids, Kiriko, to investigate the mysterious tower. Built by Mahito's granduncle, a renowned architect who vanished, the tower becomes the portal to an alternate world teeming with magic. The heron, now a guide, beckons them to enter, promising the impossible – a chance to save Hisako and Natsuko.

Once inside the tower, the trio is transported to a fantastical realm where Mahito encounters a cast of characters, each contributing to the unfolding adventure. From a seafaring version of Kiriko to Himi, a magical ally, and Warawara, bubble-like spirits embodying the cycle of life, the alternate world is a canvas of wonders.

Their quest leads them to Natsuko's granduncle, a wizard ruling the realm with formidable powers. The trio faces challenges, including a castle guarded by giant man-eating parakeets. The climactic moment arrives when they find Natsuko, who initially resists leaving until Mahito addresses her as his real mother.

Back in Mahito's world, the narrative takes an intriguing twist. A maid reveals the tower's origin – a meteorite impact and the mysterious disappearance and return of Hisako during her youth. The granduncle's character adds layers to the plot as he imparts crucial information to Mahito about maintaining balance in the magical realm.

As the story unfolds, Himi, Mahito's magical companion, is captured, leading to a confrontation with the Parakeet King. Mahito discovers the granduncle's source of power – a giant floating stone. The granduncle entrusts Mahito with the responsibility of maintaining balance, a task only someone blood-related and free of malice can undertake.

In a moment of profound choice, Mahito opts to return to his own world, acknowledging the malice within him. The consequences are dire, as the Parakeet King seeks to seize power, causing the alternate world to collapse. Amidst chaos, Mahito, Natsuko, and the heron escape, leaving behind a world on the brink of dissolution.

The emotional crescendo of the plot is reached as Mahito offers to take Himi back to his world, only to discover her true identity – a younger version of Hisako. Himi and Kiriko must return to their time to ensure Mahito's existence. The trio returns to their world, reuniting with Shoichi, marking the end of a transformative journey.

Two years later, the narrative comes full circle as Mahito, now reunited with his family, returns to Tokyo after the war's end. The film concludes, leaving viewers with a poignant reflection on the intertwining threads of loss, love, and the cyclical nature of life.

Chapter Three
Character Profiles

In "The Boy and the Heron," the characters are the heart and soul of the story, each contributing to the narrative's emotional depth and magical journey. Let's explore the key players in this cinematic masterpiece:

MAHITO MAKI:

At the heart of "The Boy and the Heron" is Mahito Maki, a 12-year-old protagonist navigating the challenges of wartime Japan. His character is a canvas of emotions, from the profound grief of losing his mother to the resilience required to adapt to a new family dynamic. Mahito's journey is a poignant exploration of loss, self-discovery, and the transformative power of magical realms.

The narrative introduces Mahito as a grieving son, struggling in a world shadowed by war. His encounters with the mysterious heron and the discovery of the sealed tower propel him into a fantastical adventure. Mahito's character arc is marked by growth, both emotional and magical, as he grapples with the complexities of his past and confronts the unknown in the alternate world.

HISAKO (Mahito's Mother):

While physically absent, Hisako's presence looms large in Mahito's life. Her untimely death shapes the narrative, driving Mahito's actions and choices. The novel "How Do You Live?" becomes a symbolic link between mother and son, offering a sense of continuity and connection beyond the boundaries of life and death. Hisako's character adds layers of emotional depth to the story, revealing the enduring impact of a mother's love.

SHOICHI (Mahito's Father):

Shoichi, Mahito's father and owner of an air munitions factory, embodies the struggle for normalcy amid wartime disruptions. Remarrying Natsuko after Hisako's death, Shoichi grapples with the complexities of blended family life. His character introduces themes of resilience and adaptation, providing a grounding element in the midst of magical realms and alternate worlds.

NATSUKO (Hisako's Younger Sister):

Natsuko steps into the role of Mahito's stepmother, bringing with her the challenges of pregnancy and the responsibilities of caring for a grieving child. Her character adds familial tension and emotional complexity to the narrative. Natsuko's connection to the magical realm, revealed through her granduncle, positions her as a bridge between the two worlds, adding layers to her character beyond the traditional stepmother role.

KIRIKO (Maid):

Kiriko, one of the maids accompanying Mahito and Natsuko, plays a crucial role in the story. As a companion on the journey to the alternate world, Kiriko provides support and guidance. Her character, with its dual existence in both Mahito's world and the magical realm, underscores the interconnectedness of the two realities. Kiriko's presence adds a touch of mystery and magical wisdom to the ensemble cast.

HIMI (Magical Companion):

Himi, a young woman with magical powers, becomes Mahito's ally in the alternate world. Unveiling her identity as a younger version of Hisako, Himi introduces a time-travel element to the narrative. Her character embodies the cyclical nature of life and the interconnectedness of past, present, and future. Himi's sacrifices and choices contribute to the emotional depth of the story, linking her fate to Mahito's existence.

PARAKEET KING:

A formidable antagonist in the alternate world, the Parakeet King adds a layer of danger and conflict to Mahito's quest. The quest to rescue Himi becomes a pivotal moment in Mahito's character development. The Parakeet King's actions, driven by a desire for power, lead to the collapse of the magical realm, underscoring the consequences of unchecked ambition.

NATSUKO'S GRANDUNCLE (Wizard):

As a wizard ruling the alternate world, Natsuko's granduncle is a key figure in the story's magical landscape.

His character introduces themes of balance and responsibility, emphasizing the delicate equilibrium required to sustain the magical realm. The granduncle's role as a mentor figure adds depth to Mahito's journey, offering insights into the interconnectedness of magical forces.

THE HERON:

A mysterious and symbolic presence throughout the narrative, the heron guides Mahito on his journey. From teasing him in the real world to serving as a gateway to the alternate realm, the heron embodies mystery and transformation. Its true nature, revealed beneath the illusion, becomes a catalyst for Mahito's choices and the unfolding of the plot.

Chapter Four
Behind the Scenes

The genesis of the film can be traced back to the mind of acclaimed director Hayao Miyazaki. Known for his visionary storytelling and ability to blend reality with fantasy seamlessly, Miyazaki embarked on a creative odyssey with "The Boy and the Heron." The initial spark for the narrative came from a desire to delve into the emotional landscapes of childhood, loss, and the transformative power of imagination.

The character of Mahito Maki, a 12-year-old grappling with the complexities of war and personal tragedy, became the focal point of Miyazaki's narrative vision. The decision to anchor the story in wartime Japan added layers of historical and emotional depth, providing a canvas for the exploration of resilience and hope amid adversity.

The animation process itself became a labor of love for the creative team. Miyazaki, known for his meticulous attention to detail, worked closely with the animators to breathe life into each frame. The choice to use traditional hand-drawn animation over computer-generated imagery (CGI) was a deliberate one, harkening back to a time when animation was a craft as much as an art form.

The team faced challenges in capturing the essence of wartime Japan authentically. Extensive research went into recreating the historical backdrop, from the architecture of Tokyo to the daily lives of its inhabitants. The result is a visually immersive experience that transports the audience to a bygone era, where the echoes of war resonate in the quiet moments of the narrative.

The creation of the alternate world, a pivotal aspect of the plot, posed its own set of challenges. The fantastical realm had to be distinct yet connected to the emotional core of the story. The design of magical creatures, landscapes, and the granduncle's castle required a delicate balance between whimsy and gravitas. The animators, led by Miyazaki's vision, crafted a world that mirrored the emotional landscape of Mahito's journey.

One of the standout elements of the film is the musical score, composed by the renowned Joe Hisaishi. The music serves as a silent yet powerful companion to Mahito's odyssey, heightening the emotional beats and adding depth to the storytelling. Hisaishi's collaboration with Miyazaki is legendary, and "The Boy and the Heron" is no exception, with a score that lingers in the hearts of the audience long after the credits roll.

Behind the scenes, the voice cast played a pivotal role in bringing the characters to life. The nuances of Mahito's grief, Natsuko's internal struggles, and the heron's mystique were conveyed through the skillful performances of the cast. The voice acting added layers of emotion and authenticity to the characters, creating a bridge between the animated world and the audience's own experiences.

In the realm of animation, where every frame is a labor-intensive creation, the dedication of the animators shines through. The fluidity of movement, the expressions that convey a myriad of emotions, and the attention to detail in every background contribute to the immersive experience of "The Boy and the Heron." The hand-drawn animation, while challenging, is a testament to the commitment of the team to preserve the artistry of traditional animation.

Chapter Five
The Voice Cast

The characters in "The Boy and the Heron" come to life not only through animation but also through the voices that give them depth and personality. The voice cast, both in the original Japanese version and the English adaptation, plays a crucial role in conveying the emotions and nuances of each character.

MAHITO MAKI (JAPANESE: SOMA SANTOKI, ENGLISH: LUCA PADOVAN):

At the heart of the story is Mahito Maki, a 12-year-old boy navigating the challenges of loss and discovery. Soma Santoki, with his expressive voice, captures the vulnerability and resilience of Mahito. In the English version, Luca Padovan brings a sincerity to the character, ensuring the emotional journey resonates with audiences.

THE GREY HERON (JAPANESE: MASAKI SUDA, ENGLISH: ROBERT PATTINSON):

Masaki Suda lends his voice to the mysterious and enigmatic Grey Heron in the Japanese version, infusing the character with a mix of allure and intrigue. Meanwhile, in the English version, Robert Pattinson's voice adds a layer of complexity, making the Heron a captivating presence in Mahito's journey.

LADY HIMI (JAPANESE: AIMYON, ENGLISH: KAREN FUKUHARA):

Aimyon, with her Japanese rendition, and Karen Fukuhara, with her English portrayal, breathe life into Lady Himi. Both versions skillfully convey the magical essence and wisdom of the character, creating a memorable presence in the alternate world Mahito discovers.

NATSUKO (JAPANESE: YOSHINO KIMURA, ENGLISH: GEMMA CHAN):

Yoshino Kimura's Japanese voice gives Natsuko a nuanced blend of strength and vulnerability. Gemma Chan, in the English adaptation, captures the internal struggles of

Natsuko, adding depth to the character's journey as Mahito's stepmother.

SHOICHI MAKI (JAPANESE: TAKUYA KIMURA, ENGLISH: CHRISTIAN BALE):

Takuya Kimura's Japanese portrayal and Christian Bale's English rendition bring forth the complexities of Shoichi Maki, Mahito's father. Both actors navigate the challenges of wartime and family dynamics, infusing Shoichi with a sense of duty and love.

GRANDUNCLE (JAPANESE: SHŌHEI HINO, ENGLISH: MARK HAMILL):

Shōhei Hino's Japanese voice and Mark Hamill's English rendition contribute to the enigmatic aura of the Granduncle. The dual performances capture the wisdom and mystery of this character, who plays a pivotal role in Mahito's journey.

KIRIKO (JAPANESE: KO SHIBASAKI, ENGLISH: FLORENCE PUGH):

Ko Shibasaki's Japanese voice and Florence Pugh's English portrayal bring Kiriko to life. Both versions encapsulate the courage and companionship that Kiriko offers Mahito on his fantastical adventure.

NOBLE PELICAN (JAPANESE: KAORU KOBAYASHI, ENGLISH: WILLEM DAFOE):

Kaoru Kobayashi's Japanese voice and Willem Dafoe's English rendition infuse the Noble Pelican with distinct characteristics. The voices convey the regality and wisdom of this mystical creature encountered in the alternate world.

THE PARAKEET KING (JAPANESE: JUN KUNIMURA, ENGLISH: DAVE BAUTISTA):

Jun Kunimura's Japanese voice and Dave Bautista's English portrayal lend a powerful presence to the Parakeet King. Both versions capture the intensity and authority of this character in the fantastical realm.

MAID CHARACTERS AND WARAWARA (JAPANESE: KEIKO TAKESHITA, JUN FUBUKI, SAWAKO AGAWA, SHINOBU OTAKE, KAREN TAKIZAWA):

The Japanese voice cast for the maid characters—Keiko Takeshita, Jun Fubuki, Sawako Agawa, Shinobu Otake—and Karen Takizawa as Warawara, contribute to the atmospheric charm of the movie. Their performances add depth to the supporting cast, enriching the world Mahito explores.

Chapter Six
Themes and Motifs

"The Boy and the Heron" is a tapestry woven with autobiographical threads, reflecting the personal experiences and sentiments of its creator, Hayao Miyazaki. The film delves into the director's own childhood, encapsulating a narrative that mirrors his family's evacuation from the city to the countryside during the war.

The protagonist, Mahito Maki, serves as a vessel for Miyazaki's memories, drawing parallels to the director's father's involvement in a company manufacturing fighter plane components, akin to Mahito's father Shoichi Maki. The poignant loss of Mahito's mother, Hisako, in a hospital fire at the film's outset resonates with Miyazaki's own bereavement, paying homage to a mother known for her strong opinions and serving as a wellspring of inspiration for the director's portrayal of female characters.

The film's central theme emerges as a coming-of-age tale, navigating Mahito's journey from selfishness to selflessness. This transformation echoes Miyazaki's own artistic evolution, deviating from his past works featuring cheerful and optimistic male protagonists. The complexity of Mahito as a character signifies Miyazaki's intent to depict boys as intricate individuals, grappling with inner conflicts and insecurities. The overarching theme, shared with Miyazaki's previous work "Kimitachi wa Dō Ikiru ka," revolves around how individuals confront and reconcile with a world marked by strife and loss.

A crucial message embedded in the narrative is the aspiration to forge "a world without conflict with your own hands." Miyazaki's faith in the potential of children to surpass previous generations, even in challenging circumstances, is encapsulated in the film's Japanese title, offering a choice between perpetuating the chaos of Japan's wartime past or charting a better course. This optimism, as The Japan Times notes, stands as a testament to Miyazaki's unwavering belief in the resilience and imagination of the younger generation.

The film invites diverse interpretations, fundamentally conveying resilience in the face of conflict and grief. It advocates for the cultivation of meaningful friendships and trustworthy alliances, promoting progress and fostering "humanity and understanding in the world." The thematic layers draw from Miyazaki's extensive body of work, departing from conventional children's genre expectations. It aligns more with the "violent" style of "Princess Mononoke" than the "cuddly charm" of "My Neighbor Totoro," signaling the film's nuanced and diverse nature.

Themes of acceptance, redemption, and the power of creation permeate the narrative, drawing explicit connections between Miyazaki's youthful inspirations and his aspiration to inspire others across decades. The juxtaposition of life and death becomes a narrative focal point, with childhood and the end of life serving as reflective counterparts. The film's exploration of moral lessons, centered on the moral development of adolescent boys, takes an open-ended approach. It becomes an impassioned plea from an aging master, the Granduncle, emphasizing the urgency of tasks as time swiftly passes.

The emotional core of the film, as recognized by Nikkei Asia, revolves around the yearning for a mother's presence, propelling the narrative into adventures involving fantastical creatures. Mahito's father's remarriage to his mother's healthier sister introduces Freudian undertones, emphasizing the child's perspective with moments of quasi-sexual elements. Despite these evocative elements, the film maintains a dreamlike quality, focusing on Mahito's mission to save his mother and stepmother—a narrative emblematic of Miyazaki's recurring theme of worthiness.

Chapter Seven
Music and Soundtrack

The musical tapestry of "The Boy and the Heron" contributes significantly to the film's emotional depth and narrative resonance. Composed by the renowned Joe Hisaishi, a long-time collaborator with Studio Ghibli and Hayao Miyazaki, the soundtrack enriches the visual storytelling, creating an immersive and evocative experience for the audience.

score seamlessly intertwines with the film's themes, enhancing the emotional impact of key scenes. The music not only complements the narrative but also serves as a powerful storytelling device, capturing the nuances of Mahito Maki's journey—from the depths of grief to the triumph of self-discovery. The composer's ability to convey complex emotions through music is evident, adding layers of depth to the characters and the overall storytelling.

One of the standout features of the soundtrack is its thematic versatility. Hisaishi masterfully employs a range of musical motifs, from melancholic and introspective melodies to uplifting and adventurous themes. This dynamic musical range mirrors the film's exploration of diverse themes, including loss, resilience, and the transformative power of personal growth.

The film's main theme, a recurring motif throughout the soundtrack, serves as a musical anchor, weaving through different scenes and tying the narrative together. This thematic consistency enhances the film's cohesion, providing a sonic thread that guides the audience through Mahito's multifaceted journey.

The orchestral arrangements, a hallmark of Hisaishi's work, contribute to the film's cinematic grandeur. The sweeping strings, poignant piano melodies, and subtle incorporation of traditional Japanese instruments create a rich sonic landscape that complements the film's visual beauty. Hisaishi's ability to seamlessly blend Western orchestration with Japanese musical elements adds a cultural depth to the score, enhancing the film's sense of time and place.

Beyond the composed score, the film's use of diegetic and non-diegetic sound elements enhances the overall auditory experience. From the rustling of leaves in the quiet countryside to the powerful soundscape of magical realms, the attention to sonic detail underscores the film's commitment to creating a fully immersive world for the audience.

The soundtrack also features a poignant vocal piece, underscoring key emotional moments in the narrative. The lyrics, when present, add an additional layer of storytelling, conveying emotions that resonate on a visceral level. This marriage of music and lyrics heightens the emotional impact of the film's most pivotal scenes.

Chapter Eight
Release and Reception

On December 13, 2022, Toho announced that "The Boy and the Heron" was set to premiere in Japan on July 14, 2023. The film marked a departure from traditional marketing strategies, with no trailers or promotional stills released before its premiere, a decision attributed to producer Suzuki.

This unconventional approach aimed to preserve an enigmatic cinematic experience, minimizing content revelation before the release. The cast and crew remained largely undisclosed until the premiere. Notably, the film saw a simultaneous release on IMAX and other high-end formats, a first for Studio Ghibli and Miyazaki.

Internationally, the film's rights were pre-sold, and GKIDS acquired the North American distribution rights.

The film had special previews on November 22 before its theatrical release in the United States on December 8, 2023. The international premiere took place at the 2023 Toronto International Film Festival, where it became the first animated film to open the festival, receiving acclaim as the "strongest opening night film in decades." Studio Ghibli granted promotional control to GKIDS for the American release, adopting a new marketing strategy to reach a wider audience while preserving Ghibli's brand integrity.

In Japan, the film achieved unprecedented box office success, grossing $13.2 million in its opening weekend, making it Studio Ghibli's biggest opening. It surpassed records set by "Howl's Moving Castle." The film continued its remarkable run, attracting over 5.17 million viewers and grossing over 7.7 billion yen ($52.9 million) within 59 days of release. By September 18, it surpassed 8.25 billion yen ($55.6 million).

The film maintained strong momentum internationally, grossing $21,770,753 across South Korea, France, Spain, Turkey, and Portugal, bringing the total gross to $77.9 million as of November 12, 2023. Journalist Hiroo Ōtaka highlighted the industry's astonishment at the film's rapid box office success, attributed in part to its unconventional marketing strategy. The deliberate minimalism generated discussion on social media, leveraging the existing fan base and indirect promotion through Ghibli's earlier works. Industry insiders expressed mixed feelings about the impact on traditional advertising methods.

The film received widespread critical acclaim. On Rotten Tomatoes, it holds a 97% approval rating, with an average score of 8.6/10. The consensus describes it as a soulful exploration of thought-provoking themes through beautiful animation, labeling it another Miyazaki masterpiece. Metacritic indicates "universal acclaim" with a score of 91 out of 100 based on 23 critic reviews.

Initial reactions were mixed, but the film quickly gained acclaim in Japan. Eiga Channel praised it as one of Ghibli's finest, emphasizing visuals and storytelling. Cinemas+ noted its darker, more complex narrative, weaving motifs and characters from Miyazaki's career. Time Out Japan hailed it as a "mature, complex masterpiece." Internationally, Caryn James of the BBC called it the culmination of Miyazaki's career, requiring multiple viewings to absorb its narrative and rich imagery.

David Ehrlich of IndieWire termed it Miyazaki's poignant farewell, graced with divine awe and heart-stopping wistfulness. IGN's Rafael Motamayor called it Ghibli's most visually complex film, delivering an exceptional conclusion to Miyazaki's career. In conclusion, "The Boy and the Heron" not only achieved remarkable box office success but also garnered critical acclaim for its unique storytelling, visual prowess, and emotional depth. The film stands as a testament to Miyazaki's ability to captivate audiences with his cinematic mastery.

Chapter Nine
Impact on Pop Culture

One of the notable impacts is the film's departure from conventional marketing strategies. By forgoing traditional promotional methods and adopting a more enigmatic approach, the film sparked discussions about the evolving landscape of film promotion. The decision to keep details under wraps until the release date generated a buzz, reflecting a departure from the information-saturated approach common in the industry.

The success of this minimalist promotion strategy has implications for the future of film marketing. The industry witnessed a blend of anticipation and curiosity, showcasing the potential for a film to thrive on its inherent merit rather than extensive promotional campaigns. This departure challenges established norms and prompts a reconsideration of how films are introduced to audiences.

Moreover, *The Boy and the Heron* has added a new chapter to the legacy of Studio Ghibli and Hayao Miyazaki. The film's exploration of darker themes, complex narratives, and personal motifs has demonstrated the studio's ability to evolve while maintaining its distinct identity. As a swan song for Miyazaki, the film serves as a reflection on his illustrious career and a testament to the enduring appeal of Ghibli's storytelling.

The film's influence extends beyond the cinematic realm, permeating popular culture through discussions in various media. Social media platforms became hubs for debates, analyses, and fan theories, amplifying the film's reach. Memorable scenes, characters, and themes became subjects of fan art, contributing to the vibrant online discourse surrounding the movie.

Additionally, the success of *The Boy and the Heron* at the box office, both domestically and internationally, signals a growing global appetite for diverse and thought-provoking animated narratives. Its triumphs set a benchmark for future animated films, emphasizing the potential for nuanced storytelling to captivate audiences worldwide.

Printed in Great Britain
by Amazon